Duke Jordan—
MORE THAN JUST AIR

DUKE JORDAN

BALBOA.
PRESS
A DIVISION OF HAY HOUSE

Copyright © 2019 Duke Jordan.

All rights reserved. No part of this book may be used or reproduced by any means, graphic, electronic, or mechanical, including photocopying, recording, taping or by any information storage retrieval system without the written permission of the author except in the case of brief quotations embodied in critical articles and reviews.

Scripture quotations marked KJV are from the Holy Bible, King James Version (Authorized Version). First published in 1611. Quoted from the KJV Classic Reference Bible, Copyright © 1983 by The Zondervan Corporation.

Balboa Press books may be ordered through booksellers or by contacting:

Balboa Press
A Division of Hay House
1663 Liberty Drive
Bloomington, IN 47403
www.balboapress.com
1 (877) 407-4847

Because of the dynamic nature of the Internet, any web addresses or links contained in this book may have changed since publication and may no longer be valid. The views expressed in this work are solely those of the author and do not necessarily reflect the views of the publisher, and the publisher hereby disclaims any responsibility for them.

The author of this book does not dispense medical advice or prescribe the use of any technique as a form of treatment for physical, emotional, or medical problems without the advice of a physician, either directly or indirectly. The intent of the author is only to offer information of a general nature to help you in your quest for emotional and spiritual well-being. In the event you use any of the information in this book for yourself, which is your constitutional right, the author and the publisher assume no responsibility for your actions.

Any people depicted in stock imagery provided by Getty Images are models, and such images are being used for illustrative purposes only. Certain stock imagery © Getty Images.

Print information available on the last page.

ISBN: 978-1-9822-1891-1 (sc)
ISBN: 978-1-9822-1893-5 (hc)
ISBN: 978-1-9822-1892-8 (e)

Library of Congress Control Number: 2018914904

Balboa Press rev. date: 01/09/2019

After it is all said and done, it is up to you to work your plan. No one will do for you what you should be doing for yourself. Get up, start walking, and never look back.

After spending some time with a few successful businessmen and women, I realized that I had been allowing the rivers of life to guide me. Now, at almost fifty-two, I have realized not only that can I take control and guide my own ship but also that I have the power to control the flow of the water in which I'm sailing. Get up this day and work your plan.

You win as soon as you stop gambling with your faith and dreams. You've got to start believing and know that you will succeed.

As soon as you stop looking at circumstances with your eyes and start knowing in your heart and mind that it is done, you've won. We all tend to default to what is easiest to see and understand. Try some blind faith today. I dare you to ask and believe that it's done.

If you want different results, you may want to try different actions. Nothing changes around you until you first make a choice within to change yourself. Don't ever forget you are here for a reason.

*F*ind that purpose in your life, align yourself with your destiny, and you will never again consider it *work*. Get up and live.

Isn't life interesting? People will sit back judging and hating on you because you are sitting in that tree stand. However, very few know about the thorns, thickets, and mud you had to crawl through to get there. They also don't realize it was you who cut the very path on which they now stand.

If you are looking for change in your life, you must first look in the mirror and ask yourself about the choices you have made thus far. It is only then, when you are honest with yourself, that you will be able to change your world. Get out of your own way.

Let this day be the first day of making that different choice. To some, it will be as simple as saying, "No—never again." To others, it will be taking an action that you should have taken years ago. Time is too valuable to continue in your present direction.

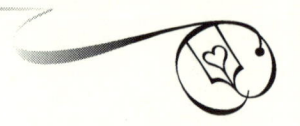

The next time you start to feel sorry for yourself, take a walk around the cemetery. Lots of dreams and choices are buried there. You still have a chance to fulfill yours and help others get to theirs. So regardless of how bad circumstances may seem, the power of choice still lives within you.

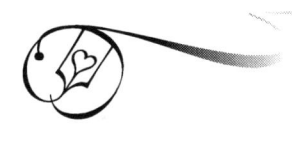

Start living today and do the very thing you've put off for years. It won't be easy, and some people may think you have lost your mind, but do it. Choose happiness and chase that dream. Don't you ever empower someone else to dictate the outcome of your circumstances. The choice is yours to make.

Sometimes God allows that whale to swallow us up for a reason. If you look back over your life, you may remember times when it seemed as though you were surrounded by darkness—but God. The whale in your life delivered you into the light and upon solid ground. Regardless of what you are going through, hold on and keep the faith. The whale that swallowed you will eventually bring a new beginning into your life.

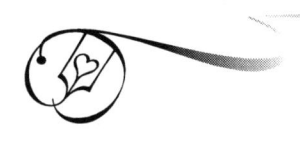

If you can gather enough crumbs, you will be able to make your own sandwich. In life, little things, no matter how small, can become much.

Sometimes you just have to take your foot off the gas, slow down, and pull into the rest area. While there, check your map to see if you are traveling in the right direction and working toward the right goals. Some of you will realize you've been heading nowhere fast. Others will realize they've been running their engine low on fuel and oil. You might be heading in the right direction, but if you don't stop every now and then to service your vehicle of life, you will not make it to your destination.

On this journey, there's nothing wrong with stopping to assist a stranded motorist. Like so many others before us, we may have to put our own destinations on hold until loved ones can drive and graduate to their personal freeways and paths. But through it all, don't ever give up. We each have our own tests to pass and destinies ahead.

What will be your life's game changer? Have you had enough self-inflicted penalties? There are plenty who would gladly stand in your shoes and feel blessed. Stop complaining about the fouls and tighten your laces. God has given each of us superior abilities and our own unique sets of skills. You've been given a brand-new day to use them. Let's get serious and win—no more excuses. Regardless of what this game of life throws our way, we can never give up. The clock has been reset. Ready ... *go*!

What is on your mind? Start paying more attention to what you are uploading to your brain. Are you reading inspirational books and looking at educational videos for development and self-help, or are you watching Vines, playing games, and following someone else's drama on social media? God has given each of us the choice of how we use our time. It is not too late to set goals and accomplish those dreams. Today, how will you choose to use your time?

It's time to work the plan. No one will do it for you. You can't do it while you sleep. Let this be the day you get up and start your journey.

As you mature in life, you will come to realize that you may not always be able to soar among the clouds and mountain peaks. In these times, remember that God has also given you feet. Start walking through your obstacles and don't give up; keep moving toward your goal.

Even though it's been a while, and prayers got you through that rough spot, Jesus is now trying to hand the wheel back to you. Take it. Yes, even though God carries us through, we shouldn't forget how to walk when he puts us down. He's always there, but we have to do our parts as well. James 2:14 says, "Faith by itself, if it is not accompanied by action, is dead."

Take that step, face your fears today, and claim the blessings that have been waiting for you to make that move. Sometimes you need to set yourself free.

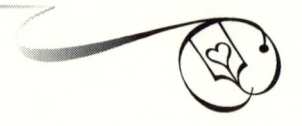

It's time to get offtrack and start cutting your own path. If you step back and look at your plan, you may realize it did not include taking the road heavily traveled to end up with most people. Your road hasn't been cut or paved. You may have the right goals in mind, but you're going to have to go off-road in your daily routine to make it there. So as you start this day, focus on changing to a more direct route to your blessing and destiny. God has already given you the talent and tools to get there. Use them to make your own road.

It is okay to lie down and dream big, but if you want your dream to come true, you need to get on your feet, work the plan, and chase it down. You also have to believe and have the faith that it's already done.

Retrain the mind, and it will affect everything around you. Your blessings are waiting for you to take the necessary actions, which God has installed in you. Manifest in your mind and believe it's already done. We all have the keys to our success within us. Use your keys to unlock yours today.

Have you thought beyond the day that you get the very thing you've been wanting your whole life? Do not measure your success by what material goods you have in your life. Today, think about someone other than yourself and what you can do to make his or her life better.

There is a true blessing in giving and doing for others. It also reflects your level of success—and not just material wealth. There are folks out there who simply need your time, knowledge, skills, companionship, friendship, and the greatest gift of all—your love. You don't have to look very far. Just open your eyes and ears. Bless them, and you will be blessed ten times over.

Don't ever let your circumstances or an obstacle decide your desired outcome. Remember you are the author of your story. Set your goals, believe, and live your life.

Whatever you do, don't ever give up on yourself. I know from my own experiences that it may seem like there's no way out or it won't get better—but God. Regardless of what your eyes may see and your ears have heard, with even a little faith, you will realize this is only a chapter. Get up and know the best is yet to come.

Greatness, abundance, healing, and blessings are waiting for us to open the door to them. That knock comes in many forms. Listen for it. I know you've heard it. Your knock may be waiting for you to bless someone else. Your knock may be you going back to school. Your knock may be waiting for you at your place of worship this morning. Whatever it may be, listen and take action. Once you make up your mind, nothing can stand between you and the blessing that has been waiting for you.

The sooner you realize that your circumstances do not dictate your outcome, the sooner you can take control of your future. Quit being a passenger and know that God is actually trying to tell some of us to take the wheel and drive. Take it, push the pedal to the floor, and get there. Simply have faith and believe that it will be done. It will be more than all right.

Death will remind us again and again that we can never take life for granted. It has shown us time and again it does not discriminate between ages. So, as we continue down this road called life, I can only hope that God will give those who are going through a recent loss a peace and understanding that surpasses all the circumstances they are facing. I do believe no parent should have to bury a child, but I also believe God has a plan that's bigger than you and me. Everything happens for a reason. Find it, and you'll find that peace awaits you there as well. Condolences to all the families who are suffering from a recent loss. Don't ever give up.

Thoughts and ideas can be great, but nothing will change until you develop your plan and turn it into actions. Proper actions set us on course toward the success that has always been there waiting for our arrival. Today is a good day to start. It is never too late. For those of you who have been knocked down, get back up and fight for what you know is already yours.

lost a deal yesterday. I tell you this because it is simply making me dig in deeper and get ready for the next battle. We cannot sit back and drown in our tears and fears over a few lost battles. The war is not over. If there's one thing I know for sure, it's that I am winning the next one. If we stay focused and believe, we will win our personal wars. Regardless of whether you get up or dig in, it is not over. You must take action to see victory. Have a wonderful day.

Follow your plans to reach your goals while not conforming to what others say and do, and your dreams will chase after you. Faith is the missing element for so many of us. We have to start believing and know that it's done before seeing it. For some of us, all we have to do is simply reach out and grab it. Your blessing is waiting for you to act. Your works have brought it to your doorstep. Open the door.

Only a few haters will care about your past mistakes. We all have them. You have to move on and do what you know is right for you and your family. Don't look back. What will you do today? It's time.

If you truly want to take it to the next level, you're going to have to get uncomfortable. We all tend to go through life wondering why the Gateses and the Oprahs seem to have it all. Folks like them have gotten uncomfortable by taking those risks. If you want different results or outcomes in your life, you first have to change your mind-set and actions. Your harvest will always be a direct reflection of what you have sown. For those of you who are about to give up, hang in there. Your harvest is just around the corner.

To those who feel like giving up, and to those who think they will never make it through, God has hidden in each of us an extra battery pack full of faith and strength into which we can connect. All you have to do is believe and continue working destiny's plan for your life. Yes, most of our lives' plans have been written. Once you come into alignment with them, your real story of true success begins.

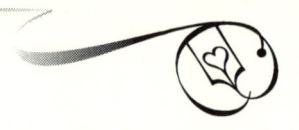

Just remember, you can't always measure one's success by the amount in their bank account. Many of your stories of success will simply be making it through a certain period of your life with a loved one's life or your life. Don't ever give up on you. Today, stand up and plug into your extra battery pack.

In your darkest days, still be thankful. Keep moving forward with faith. The skies will eventually open and reveal the sun that has always been present. Think about it. You may have crawled through the dark, but you never got cold. Even through our own personal hells, blessings still surround us. Have a great day and look up.

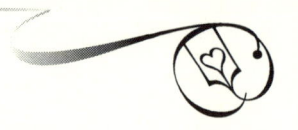

At the end of the day, we are all in life's river, en route to the same end. The difference is how we are navigating it. Some of us are floating in a rubber raft, while others seem to be on a cruise ship, 365 days of the year. The question is, If your raft is sinking, how do you change your mode of transportation? Are you willing to get wet on your own terms? Yes, sometimes life simply gives you that ticket to walk onto the cruise ship while it's docked, but most of us have to fight to gain entry.

Do you have a plan in place to take you to your desired location, or are you allowing the current to take you where it wants you to go? Some of us will almost drown, risking everything for a better raft, while others will see the water coming in and depend on others to save them. On this day, who will you be? Will you be a fighter for a better tomorrow, or will you become waterlogged and slip into the murky deep? I applaud those who are building their own rafts and ships. Regardless of your situation, don't ever give up on you. I know it's hard, but even if you have slipped beneath the surface, start kicking and reach up. Help is always there.

As wisdom and age set in, you come to realize it's not all about you; nor is it about the "I" accomplishments. Living life to its fullest is about loving one another and helping others reach their goals. In doing so, your cup will always overflow with blessings.

We all have times when we will feel like our name is Job. It is during those tests and trials we have to know and believe that everything will be all right.

Even though you don't know how, and you may not see the way, you will make it through stronger and better. Anyone can lie around feeling depressed and sorry for themselves. I dare you to get up and start giving thanks as if it were already done.

Even though you may be going through your own storms of hell, you can still be a blessing to get someone else through their own. If you can hold your breath longer and are a better swimmer, be that life vest or line to get someone else on the boat before you. In this world of karma, they may just be the key to getting you to your destination. The key is not doing it and expecting something in return but doing it just because you can.

I thank God above for second chances. Just as the first, what you do with it is up to you. Some are blessed to see their thirds and fourths. Just remember, this may be your last chance to get it right.

Today, as you go out into the world, live as though this is your last. Treat those around you as if you will never see them again. If you can do something kind anonymously for someone, do it. I'm a living witness that karma does exist. Have a wonderful day.

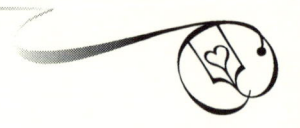

Good morning. It's going to be a great day. Regardless what has come our way, we are still here. Yes, we may be a little older and unable to perform handsprings, but we are still here. I know how it feels to be overwhelmed and stressed with multiple cares of this world. It is in those times that you must buckle down, stay the course, and know that no one can stop God's blessings or plans for your life but you.

Remember you can only overdraw so much out of your prayer bank account that someone else has supplied for you until you have to start putting in some of your own time on your knees. Have a blessed day.

You cannot expect change in your life while you are sitting there doing the same things. You have to be the change before you can expect anything else to change in your world.

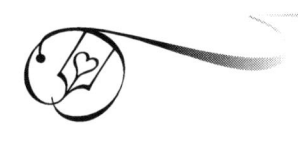

We sometimes wonder why we must go through so many storms. The storms come to wash away the debris of hopelessness you are holding. They come to uproot those who are telling you it's all right to settle for seconds. They come to give you an opportunity to reset your position and rearrange your priorities. The storm will blow it all away and give you a chance to truly see yourself. You will finally realize there are those around you who love you and will help you by providing the tools and knowledge to reach the top.

Have you ever noticed how even the air we breathe after a storm seems so pure and refreshed? If you are in a storm, embrace it. It's nothing less than an opportunity for transition. Take a deep breath and make the decision.

We all have an important part to play in this journey called life. In the end, don't you want to be able to look back and say you had no regrets? In your life, there is still time to eliminate the would've and should've. There is no better time than now to make that decision to get it done. If that "it" is working well in your life, then help someone else solve the "it" in their life. Do it not for the praise but because you can.

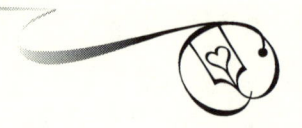

Sometimes, before blaming others for the situation, we have to take a look in the mirror and make sure the person looking back at us is doing everything they are supposed to be doing.

Hang in there. Help is on the way. It may not show up in the form you thought it would, but be still and know that it's coming.

Yes, it's all worth it. Sometimes you have to separate what feels good from what you know is right. Even if you're feeling numb to your actions, if they are the rights ones, it will all work out. Hang in there. Weekends can produce new tests, add fuel to a fire, and play on insecurities. Don't fall for it and don't give up on yourself.

Don't ever let someone's negative input affect the positive outlook of your future. Your first mistake was listening to them in the first place, and your second was believing it. Reboot your mind and find your purpose.

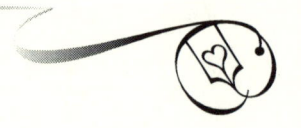

Yes, a choice can be made in seconds, but true change occurs over time. You didn't get those ways or habits overnight; therefore, even after you make that choice, don't expect instant results. Real habits and addictions, good or bad, are hard to break.

Remember, attached to the one with much wisdom and knowledge is a chapter in their lives of pain, sacrifice, and mental scarring. It just takes some of us longer to finish that chapter than others. If you are stuck in a bad chapter of your life, make the choice to start on the next. Only you can turn the page into a different tomorrow. You already know what you shouldn't or should be doing. Get it done.

I believe it's going to be a productive day for a lot of us. You may just get what you've been needing or an answer to that prayer. From head up, to feet on the ground, expect your blessing. Regardless of how it appears or the negative reports you've gotten, don't give up. Whatever it is, just add "—but God" after it. The best thing is, for it to work, you don't have to be anywhere near perfect. Beware of the haters disguised as your friends and supporters.

A true blessing is helping or doing something for someone else, expecting nothing in return, just because you can. In serving others, you may just find the secret to your own breakthrough. Yes, in this human race, you can finish first, but after crossing your finish line, wouldn't you like to encourage and help others who are still running the race?

There can only be so much planning and thinking about it. It's time to go for it. We've been through too much and come too far to give up now. It's our time. Speak it, claim it, and take what has always been yours.

Today I made myself a couple of promises. Sometimes in our lives, we need to step back and take an inventory of not only the people in our lives but also our thoughts. We can be so much more. It's easy to make the decision, but a lot of us fail when it comes to taking action. Take action today.

You are going to fall down. You are going to fail. You may even have a total breakdown while trying. It's all part of life's great journey. You don't have to stay down. You don't have to continue in failure. It is you who is holding yourself back. It is you who is making excuses. It is you who has given up on yourself. As I look back over my life, I realize my rising up from my test began in my mind and was followed by completing the necessary actions. Get out there and put those plans into action. If you feel like you're facedown or backed against a wall, get up.

Yes, it would be nice if it was just handed to us, but sometimes we have to fight for our blessings. Sometimes the blessing is enduring the struggle. It's time to put your decisions into action. Don't look back and don't ever give up. Sprinkle a little faith on those actions and stand by. It's all going to be all right.

𝓕ailure can only mean success is just around the corner. We've got to refuse to let a couple of losings battles dictate the outcomes of our personal wars. Just because you get knocked on your back doesn't mean the fight is over. One of the best fighters I know, like Ted Malone, can take you to school while lying on his back. This week, regardless of your position, fight for your success. You have to know that everything will be all right.

We are seeing no respect for one another and no respect for life slowly infest and kill America. The lack of love and respect for one another is our greatest enemy and challenge to overcome. We all need to examine our hearts. As West Virginian citizens, our test will come. Will we be ready to handle it, or will it tear us apart? I, for one, am here if anyone ever needs an ear. Let's not give up on one another. I hope this is the day you truly start living.

Just because you are going through your own hell doesn't mean you can't reach out and help someone through their storm. It will be more than just all right. Don't you ever give up. Help is on the way in ways you couldn't have imagined.

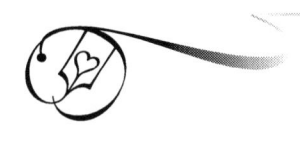

I don't know about you, but I'm sick and tired of seemingly reliving the same ole day over and over. It's time for a change. Most of us already know the root of our downfalls. We even know the answers to our problems. So, if we know what we should be doing to claim our blessing, why don't we just reach out and grab it? It's already yours. Upon awakening tomorrow, I'm going to push through and claim mine. How about you? Giving up is not an option.

As you lie down tonight and get up tomorrow, make that decision to be victorious, instead of drowning in stress. Instead of letting it immobilize your mind, choose to move toward your goal. Even as you come to what looks like a dead end, push through. You may have to cut and create your own path. Regardless of where you are in your journey, don't give up on yourself. It will be more than just all right. It is never too late.

I've had one of those working one hundred miles per hour, sun up to stars out type of weeks. I've missed phone calls, messages are full, and I have enough paperwork to do to choke a pig. Every now and then, you simply have to put it all on hold and regroup. I should be back on track tomorrow.

Actions without a plan can lead to feeling overwhelmed. You have to plan your work and work your plan. Organizing a definite plan of action and sticking to it can be the missing link to your success. There can be no room for procrastination. Get up and let's get to work.

Good morning. Today, let's get it right. No more excuses for wasting time. No use thinking about the yesterdays and the should haves. Taking the lessons of the past and applying them to your present will redefine your future. Some of you have been given the tools and talents to change the world around you. Use them. No one can hold you back but you.

You can decide to just sit there and give up because of the bad news or after failing once or twice, or you can get out there today knowing everything is going to be all right. You simply have to choose. When you look back over your life, you will realize you've always had the power of choice. Choose wisely.

If we can only remember that none of us are perfect, and all of us have something in our lives, past or present, of which we are not so proud. So the next time you go judging and condemning someone to hell, stop and think about your own experiences. Think about how blessed you are to have that second, and some of us fourth or fifth, chance to get it right. Don't let anything on this earth or anything sent from the depths of hell stop or turn you around from your blessing that awaits just around the corner. We've come too far to turn back now. I'm believing and praying that tomorrow will bring that blessing or long sought-after change in all of our lives. Simply ask for it and believe.

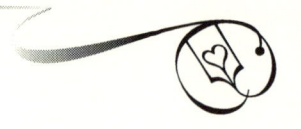

How will people remember you after you're dead and gone? What kind of memories are you working on for the future? We each hold the keys to our destiny. It all comes down to you putting them in that locked door and turning the knob. No one can do it for you. If you embrace your destiny and purpose, it's hard to tell how many books and movies will make mention of your name. You are the only one who can stop you. It's never too late.

Regardless of your storm, you are an example of what I talk about. Keep up the fight. We may never know why to some of life's storms, but we need to realize God does have a purpose and plan for us all. I'll keep you in my prayers.

When you get to the point where you think you can't go on, and the storm starts to blow you down, crawl toward your goal. No one said it would be easy. The storm will pass, and the winds will cease to blow. Once you stand on your feet again, you'll realize some of the folks who were around you are no longer there; the storm has removed them from your life. There is a cleansing side to all the storms in our lives. If you look back over your storms and really think about what you went through, you will see how the storm removed that very thing you thought you had to have and replaced it with what you were supposed to have in the first place. Don't ever give up on you. Expect more.

If you want success, failure should not be an option, regardless of how hard it gets. You may have to regroup. You may have to rest for a while. To get on the right path, you may even have to take a few steps backward. Just know that as long as you don't give up or become complacent, you will make it. It's great having others believe in your abilities, but until you start believing in yourself, it means nothing. Use the talent God has given you and make it happen.

Today, take the action to make it happen. We've all been blessed with the ability to do so. Some of you have been waiting for answers for far too long. You've had the key all along. Believe in yourself and trust in your God-given abilities and talents. No one can stop you but you.

I truly believe if we all step up our faith just a notch, those doors that were slammed shut in our faces will fly open. For some of you, all you have to do is turn the handle and walk through. Your blessing awaits. We all have a purpose. Find yours, and happiness will seek you. There's power in believing. Don't you ever give up.

Our faith will be tested. We'll never grow without tests. Regardless of what comes or goes, regardless of delays, I'm going to press through. This day, what decision will you make? The struggles in life are real, but by keeping our eyes fixed on our goals, we shall make it through these test and trials. Look up and don't ever give up. Have a great day.

I am reminded today of how some wait until a birthday or holiday to show love or give thanks to close friends or family—me included. Before the next funeral, it's not too late to reach out to those you haven't seen or to whom you haven't spoken.

Regardless of our circumstances or what has come and gone, our mothers should be at the center of our worlds. They have given us what no other person could give—life and unconditional love. So, to all of the moms out there, thank you for loving us and never giving up on us. Today, what will you do with the gift of life given to you?

Good morning! Hope you have a great day. Just remember we are the only ones who can hold ourselves back from prosperity. It's right there. Some of us just have to work harder for it.

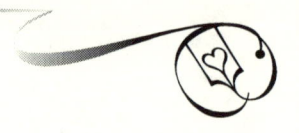

You have to keep pushing through to your goal. If you're giving it all you've got, and it seems as though you're not getting anywhere, don't give up. Keep your legs moving and keep your eyes on the goal line. Remember, when it comes to encouragement or advice, the best may come from where you least expect it, even a hater. Some of your so-called friends do not want you to climb the ladder of success. There's a lot of truth in "He will make thine enemies your footstools." You're going to make it.

The next time it seems as if there is no way out and life is drowning you, be still for a second. You might just realize you've been swimming in the wrong direction. Get out there today and swim smarter, not harder. Don't let anyone tell you you're not going to make it.

We all have come to that intersection where we have the choice to continue in our same direction or turn left or right. I can testify that, in my own life, I have pulled some complete U-turns. Some of us never even realize that we have the power to steer in one direction or the other; we're just along for the ride with an unknown destination. It's time to reach up and grab the steering wheel.

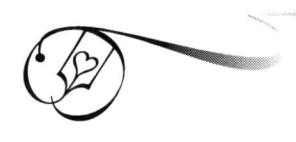

As you go through the rough roads in life, you sometimes have to have a four-wheeling mentality. In those times, you need to lock it in four-wheel drive, drop it in low gear, and drive through it. I know it doesn't look like you'll make it through, but I'm here to tell you that you will make it. If you get stuck, just attach your winch to some good old faith and scripture to pull you free. Regardless of what storms come and go, you've got to know and believe you shall make it to your destination.

Only you can make the decision that leads to failure or success. We each have been given special tools to map out and follow the plan of success in our lives. Our only holdup is actually sticking to the decision after making it. It's not always easy, but if it was, everyone would be doing it. Hang in there and keep doing what you know is right for you and your loved ones.

The next time you find yourself putting in time worrying about the tomorrows that haven't come and the past that you will never change, remember this: that on which you think the most will come into existence. Thinking about the stress will lead to more stress. Thinking about the lack of something will lead to less of what you already have. You do not have the time or energy to spend on thinking about the negatives in this life.

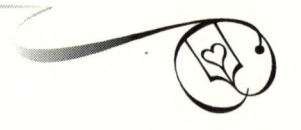

Today, you have to make a change in your life. Don't look back and definitely don't look down. Look in the mirror, and you will see that your answer has been staring you right in the face. You have been given the power to change your life. Now quit making excuses and looking for someone else to do it. Get it done.

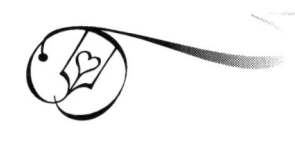

It's taken a while, but I finally realized we can be our own worst enemies. As I look back over my life, I've seen the periods of darkness and hopelessness to which my choices contributed. We become so used to picking up apples off the ground that we miss all the blessings hanging above our heads. We've got to start reaching up and grabbing them.

Some of you are double qualified to have a position, but you're waiting for someone to give it to you. Take it or start your own business. Some of us are wondering why the more we make, the less we have. It's our choices. God has given each of us special tools and talents to be successful. We simply have to decide to use them in the right way.

Wishing you a great day. Get out there and make it happen. You'll have some obstacles that get in your way, but don't let them (most of the time, him or her) stop you. You'll make it. After arriving, don't forget from where you came. Remember, there were times in your life when someone else kept you from giving up; they were that helping hand in the time of your storm.

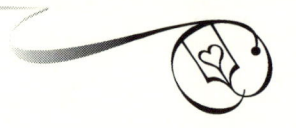

We have all fallen short at one time or another. Think back on your life and check your closets before ripping someone else's doors open. Life is a journey, and believe it or not, we are all in it together. There's nothing we can't do as a people working in one accord. It is time for West Virginians to come together and demand results for their state as a whole. What will you do in your state to change the face of the nation? It just takes one to light the fire within many.

In spite of your present circumstances, just hold on. Sometimes the only thing to say is, "But God."

Sometimes, just as the caterpillar, you will have to be still before your transformation takes place. Some of you don't even know you're supposed to be flying because you have gotten comfortable hanging out with the other caterpillars who are also crawling and inching around. I believe all of us have been given special abilities that will allow us to soar among the successful.

Good morning! I hope you get up and get it done today. Let's do something great—even better if we can do it for someone else.

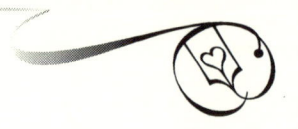

Regardless of what you're going through, don't get stuck in it. Get through it and don't look back. One of the most important things to remember as a motorcycle rider is to look where you want to go; the motorcycle will automatically follow. If you look at that guardrail in a turn, you're going to eat it up. If you focus on the pothole, you'll hit it every time. Quit focusing on the obstacles and see your way around them. Keep your eyes focused on where you want to be. You will make it happen and reach your destination.

Regardless of how gloomy, wet, and cloudy it may seem, rise above it all, and you will see that the sun is still shining on us all. Just because you can't see how in the world you're going to make it through doesn't mean you're not going to make it. Dig deep and grab a little more faith. This storm in your life shall pass. For some, it's a financial storm, and for others, it may be a relationship storm. Regardless of what type of storm you are going through, just hang in there. Don't ignore that friend who's trying to give you an umbrella or raincoat. Just because you're in the rain doesn't mean you have to get wet.

If you ever think it's so bad that you can't go on, please call someone. If they don't answer, I may not have the answer, but I'll listen. Are we not just one big family? We've got to be there for one another. Choose life and live it. It will be all right, regardless of how it appears. Just don't ever give up on you.

The longer you sit there and think about giving up, the more time you waste. Regardless of how gloomy it may appear, quit thinking about your present situation and look ahead at what is to come. Regardless of how dark the skies may be, the sun is still shining brightly. We simply have to rise above our personal storms. I know I haven't gotten this far to turn back now. The best is yet to come—for all of us.

Today, have a little faith. What you've been waiting for is just around the corner. Today, some of you will get your good news or see the results of your hard work. Make sure you tell the rest of us about it when it happens or when you get the news. It has not been in vain.

It's a great week to do something that will affect, in a positive way, someone else's life forever. I've been on this earth long enough to know it does all come back around. If you're planting seeds of hate and hopelessness, it will come back to you ten times worse. Just because you don't see it happening doesn't mean it's not happening behind closed doors or within someone.

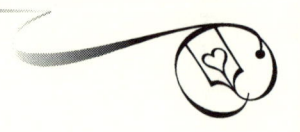

We all have personal journeys we have to travel. Some of you are destined for greatness, if you would only step out of your own way.

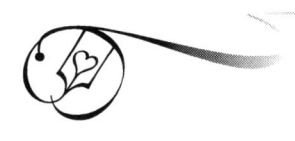

Quit holding yourself back and blaming others for your failures. Get up and make this week the week you will look back on, saying, "I made up my mind to make it and started on my way to success." No one can stop you but you. Once you've made it, don't forget about those of us who are yet in the battle but heading in the right direction. Help, not handouts, are always good. I'll see you on the streets this week.

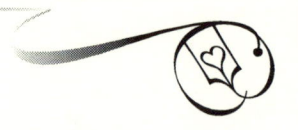

Life can be rough. You may feel as though the waves are knocking you down, one right after another, and you're stuck in the same place. We all encounter riptides in life's journey. Simply change your direction. Quit fighting it. It doesn't mean you will not reach your destination. It simply means you are going to have to take an alternate path.

For years, some of you have just treaded water and floated. You're surviving but not truly living. You are actually going backward. It's time to change your direction and swim strokes until you reach that goal. Don't you even think about giving up. Once you've reached your destination, be that lighthouse to others who may have lost their way.

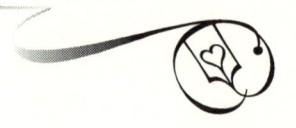

Sometimes it's easier to blame others rather than admitting you're your own worst enemy. Quit blaming others for the decisions you are making. Make the one that you know is right and watch the positive changes take place in your life and in the lives around you. I didn't say it would be easy, but you already know what choice should be made.

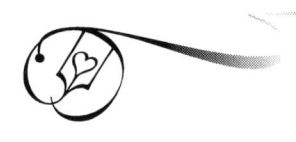

As you approach the new year, remember there is no use in making the decision to change paths and just stand still. If you've made that decision, start walking down that path until you reach the pavement and don't look back. You may have to get dirty. You might even get cut by a thorn or two. You just might have to crawl under or over that obstacle. But in the end, as long as you don't give up, you're going to make it.

And so the day begins. Good morning. Today, get out there and do something special for a complete stranger, just because you can. Even a kind word may be just what they need.

Who is without stain in their lives? Who can actually say that if the light was turned on and the Memorex was rolling, they would be proud of every moment? To those who actually can walk on water and raise the dead, I applaud you. For the rest of us, let's examine ourselves before casting bricks and stones.

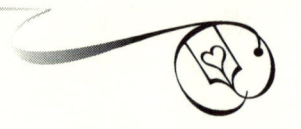

Any fool can join a cause because everyone else is doing it, but it takes real men and women to stand on their own because of what they feels is right.

Regardless of how the situation appears right now, it's going to work out. Some of you may be thinking there's no way out or *I just can't*. Hang in there. You've come too far to give up now. Faith is not just believing but knowing all will work out. Again, don't you give up.

It is a good day to do that very thing you know you should have been doing for a long time. For others, it may be the day you stop doing that which has put you in your present status. You didn't reach this place overnight, but right now you can make the choice that will put you on a different path to positive change and success. It doesn't mean all the tears of sorrow will forever disappear. There will always be those days. That's just life. However, there is comfort when you believe, have faith, and know what the end will bring in this life.

On this day, start living, choose to stick around, and tell your story of how you were just an empty vessel. I'm not going to preach because I'm a long way from walking on water. Heck, there was a time the boat would have sunk if I stepped into it. If you've tried everything else, and everything else has failed, try God. He is truly a different path to success.

Did anyone else have to push themselves out of bed this morning? This week has been nothing but morning to midnight of working. Most of us work too hard not to have everything that we want, but of course, God continually blesses us with all our needs, even when we don't deserve it. You know that whatever you've done, you can't change it, but you can change your choices from this moment forward.

It's time to take whatever you are doing to the next level. It's time to start doing that very thing you think it is too late for you to do. It is never too late. Quit looking out the window at others, as if you are stuck in your situation. The door of opportunity is already open. All you have to do is step through it into the blessing that's been waiting for you.

𝓔very now and then, you need someone on which to lean. Who is that person in your life? If you start looking around and don't have that go-to person(s), you may want to start doing a little self-examining. You may have pushed the ones who loved you most away in your times of confusion. You can still reach out to those true friends, but don't be surprised if they are a little gun-shy. We are all human and have our own individual problems that may haunt us in one or more ways. Just remember that when that person in need is looking for a shoulder on which to lean or an ear to listen. We do so much better when we help one another. It all comes around.

A dream without a plan is only a dream. Put your plan into action and start working on making your dreams a reality. Don't give up. The only person who can get in your way is you doubting yourself.

What will you do for someone else today that may change their life or situation? For some of you, it's as simple as a word, a phone call, or the stroke of a pen.

Life is so precious. Some don't get a second chance. Some don't get to choose whether to live or die. To those of you feeling as though you can't go on and that life has dealt you all the wrong cards, stop. Quit feeling sorry for yourself and do what you know you should have done years ago.

We've all been through or are going through our own personal struggles or demons. We wear them differently. Regardless of how bad it may seem, remember you're never alone. You will soon notice that the sun has never stopped shining; it was that you chose to come out only at night. Wake up, snap out of it, and step into the light.

Nothing good can come from worrying and stress. So why do we spend so much time with them? Rebuke it, and in spite of your situation, spend more time giving thanks for what you have. The answer is never in the form of a pill, bottle, or illegal substance. Yes, they have their time and place, but you have to make that choice to find yourself once again and stand.

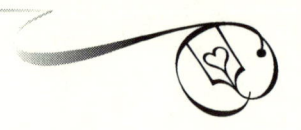

𝒥 know it's not easy, but I've read, "He will not put more on you than you can bear." Don't even think about giving up. Pray for your breakthrough and then believe that it's coming.

How do you know if you haven't tried? If you failed, try again. Just don't give up on yourself. Anything that's worth anything will require putting in some time and making sacrifices. Now get out there and knock it out of the park, or at least get a base hit. Determination and consistency will get you to home plate.

The dreams of your tomorrows will depend on the work and effort you put into the reality of your todays.

I can truly see the end of this tunnel. Sometimes we may not understand why we had to go through it in the first place. Do you ever think about why tunnels are made? They are built to provide protection around you as you go through those mountains in your life. I'm thankful for the tunnels through which I've traveled. I'm also grateful for the changes they have made in my life. Next time, before complaining, remember that tunnels may be just what you need at this time in your life to see you through.

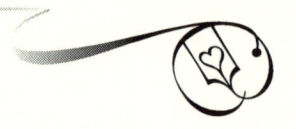

It's time. No one else can do it. No more excuses. Once you decide to move forward with it, no one can stop you except you. Choice is a powerful thing that we all possess.

Don't forget: that very thing that you pursue the most just might catch you. Do you really know what you are chasing? Every now and then, slow down long enough to ask yourself, "Do you really want it?"

It's when it seems that you can't go on that you need to make that decision to believe and fight for it. Some never thought you'd make it this far, but you're still in the race. Don't ever give up.

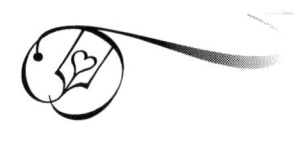

Learn to celebrate with others when they are blessed, instead of wondering why you haven't gotten yours. Quit judging, hating on them, and thinking they aren't worthy. The last time I checked, we all have room for improvement. I know I'm still working on me.

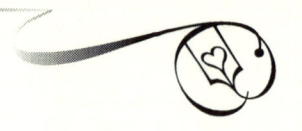

Today, let us all work on loving thy neighbor. It's a great start to healing and bringing our communities together as one.

How many more excuses will you give for not doing what you know you should be doing? How much more time will be wasted on going in circles? Today is a good day to start on that choice you've made time and again but failed to follow through on. Some of us work too hard and too many hours not to have some of the things we want. How about you? Sometimes it's as simple as reaching out and grabbing it or walking through the door. It's been open all along.

You can make this day like every other day over the past few months or years, or you can simply make that choice to take positive action that will create change in your life and in the lives of those around you. No one can stop you or hold you down but you and your decisions.

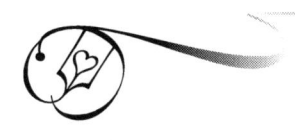

I was about to complain when I realized I've got every reason to be giving thanks for the opportunity to enjoy yet another day. I thought about all the things in life we all take for granted. I was going to complain about working so hard yet seemingly having less than others. I thought back on my days as a police officer, on all the suffering and true victims. I started thinking about those I grew up with who aren't here with us any longer. Well, it only took me a minute to realize that I have no right to complain. Do you?

The fire is not only meant to burn; the fire is needed to take out the impurities in our lives. There's always a story to share for those who have been through it. Some of us need to burn some things in our lives. Some of us need to spread a little fire on that situation that has held us hostage for years. Some of us need to take a torch to those mental chains that have held us down for too long. For some, it will take only a spark, and for others it will be a lightning strike that starts the fire. I'm breaking out the matches this week. I'll share the matches if you need some fire in your life.

Today, try saying no to that one thing that is dragging you down or destroying a relationship, or the thing that will kill the rest if you don't do something about it. Only we know who we truly are inside and out. Break that chain that is holding you down. Throw out those thoughts that have held you captive for so long. Make that decision to start living again—right now. Don't be fooled into thinking it will be perfect here on out. It took some of you months or years to get into that situation or mind-set. It will take time before you are completely back on track.

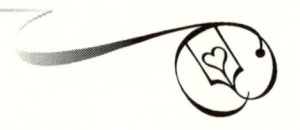

Don't drag your feet. You know good and well you're the only one who can get it done—and get it done right. Stop complaining about it; you know you're the one standing in your way.

So, your boat is sinking. God has given some of you the ability to fix it, while others he's given a whole new boat. Either way, you've got to act before you sink.

Quit wondering why everyone else appears to be happy twenty-four hours a day and to have an abundance in their bank account. We each have our own trials and secret hells. It is how we respond to them that makes us who we are. Get up, get up, get up and do what you know you should have already done. The answer is right there.

When you think you've reached the end of your rope, turn on some music, give thanks for what you have, try to laugh more, and help others if you can. In helping someone else through their hard times, you will rise above your own problems. When you give thanks, even in the bad times, your blessings will be increased. Have a great day, my friend.

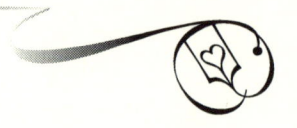

That very thing you focus on the most will come into existence. If you are constantly focused on not having enough, you will never have enough. If you focus on not having that right person in your life, you will never have them in your life.

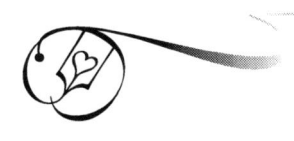

Be thankful for what you have right now. Some would consider it a blessing. I know we all have different definitions of *happiness* and *enough*, but I also know that most of us are quick to complain about what we don't have. Upon awakening to another day, be thankful that you're able to get up. Try doing something for someone else. It's not all about you all the time. Your blessing will come when you least expect it, and you'll never imagine from whom.

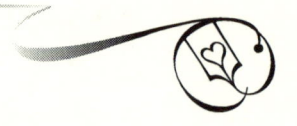

You've been given another day. Time for that decision. What will yours be? No one can do it for you. It is time for you to pick yourself up, brush yourself off, and get out there and get it done. I've never seen complaining, without actions, truly get anyone anywhere.

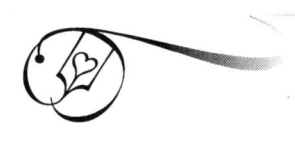

You can sit back and keep hating on those who seem to do less work yet have it all, or you can get off your butt and be determined to change your situation. Don't wait until Monday. If you're hungry, there are no weekends or holidays—only time and opportunity. So while others may be sleeping in from partying or enjoying their well-deserved weekend, I know what I've got to do. I'm still hungry and determined. I'll see you out there.

Pills and heroin have destroyed and taken thousands of lives. Just like cocaine, other drugs don't care about the color of your skin, how wealthy you are, your job title, or your physical address. It's simply an addiction tool of the devil that comes to kill, steal, and destroy one's hopes of a better tomorrow. Some of you, right now, may be looking for that next hit or escape. It is up to you to stop the cycle. It is your choice to take another path to cope with that depression, pain, anger, or hopelessness. You can make it through this. Just open your eyes, and you'll realize that help is all around you. Yes, even those family members from whom you've stolen. Love and forgiveness are stronger than anything you've ever done.

This day, make that choice not to continue full speed ahead to physical, financial, and family destruction. While I'm on the subject, addictions come in many forms. In examining ourselves, each of us will find something to which we are or were addicted. We must ask ourselves, In what ways is it affecting those around us? If it is negative, think about what is more important to have in your life. Even though it may have a chokehold on you, reach up; someone will be there to pull you up and away from it. You simply have to make the choice to reach.

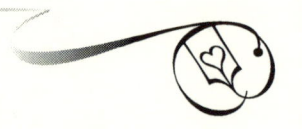

All of your work, struggle, and sacrifice is not in vain. Hang in there, keep the faith, and the end result is going to blow your mind. Don't give up now. Keep working on your story. The final chapter is yet to be written.

Don't ever depend on someone else to tell you that you are worth more. Don't fall into that cycle of mental and physical abuse. It can be a vicious cycle of depending on that very one who has stripped you of all self-identity and security. You know who you are, and most of the time, your closest friends and family do as well. That's another reason they make you stop talking to them. At the end of the day, they have total control of your life. Couples, love and respect each other. If you're staying out of fear, know that you're not alone, regardless of your mind-set. There is someone out there who will love you just the way you are. Some of you knew it was over years ago, before the pregnancy. Quit using the kids as game pieces. Believe it or not, they do have feelings and needs. They aren't as stupid as you think. Karma will catch up with you.

Although beautiful, some people can be like uncontrolled ivy, smothering, suffocating, and killing everything on which it grows. At times, even beauty has to be controlled to prevent its roots from strangling you. Men and women, be respectful to each other. It's never too late to cut back the ivy and love again.

Remember, when it comes to time, we are nothing more than a speck of dust, affecting only a small sphere of those in and around us. In the future, when historians look back, will anyone be able to locate your impressions on the lives of others? What will the tomorrows reveal about our todays? If you are still on this earth, it is for a reason.

Find that purpose, and you will find your destiny. We've all made mistakes and bad decisions, but only you have the power and choice to start making the right ones in your life. The mental connections of affairs, the power of addiction, the hatred, and depression didn't happen overnight, nor will they disappear in a day. It will take time to, once again, establish your new baseline of life, but you can make that decision to start or change right now. Yes, today truly can be that day you started living. True, we are all simply specks of dust, but we do have the power of now, with choices to make this day that could affect one or millions.

Regardless of how it may seem and look, hang on. You're almost there. Your purpose will be revealed to you. The ones against you and talking about you most realized it a long time ago. Don't pay attention to the negatives and naysayers and fall into that trap. God has a plan for all of us. Keep your head up and stay focused.

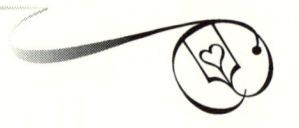

When it comes to time, quit worrying about quantity and start focusing on the quality of it. It will make a difference. The time we've spent worrying and stressing is gone. Not every day is going to be sunny, but as long as you are here, you have choices over your todays and tomorrows. Now would be a good time to put it in gear and move from that spot where you've kept yourself. No more excuses, and remember no one is perfect. "Let he who is without sin cast the first stone." I don't see any rocks flying. Do you?

Some will go for it and get it done, while others will waste time thinking about how to get it done, who else needs to be involved, and how hard it will be. Today, in which category will you fall?

*E*ven when you're walking through your own Valley of the Shadow of Death, the Word says, "I will fear no evil, thy Rod and Staff, they comfort me." Who or what, in your time in the valley, is your rod and staff? When you find them or it, you'll find comfort and peace in the midst of the storm. Most of the time, the answer is right in front of you. "Seek and you will find. Ask and it shall be given unto you." Sometimes you'll have to kick the door down if it doesn't open after knocking. Regardless of how it appears or what you've been told, hold on and don't give up. What you've been waiting for is just up ahead.

I can't help but notice, after a storm, the cleansing of the air and dusting of the trees and flowers. In life, sometimes we too need a storm or two to reset our path. You can't see it while you're in it, but you'll come out a stronger and wiser person, ready for growth. Don't give up on yourself. Your storm will pass.

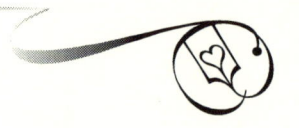

Time to settle in and get business right. We all have our defeats. It's how you react and come out on the other side that determines whether or not you are a winner. We've got to keep moving forward, regardless of what or who may come and go. There's a winner in all of us. Get your head up and set your eyes back on that goal. Don't ever give up. It will come to pass.

Some come out of their tunnel and are blinded by the light. They then decide to repeat the cycle of returning to their place of darkness and comfort—the tunnel. Stay in the light and allow yourself to adjust. It won't always be easy, but in the end, it'll be worth it.

Someone needs to know that the easiest thing to do is give up on yourself and life. It may seem as though it has been thought out, but in their mind, nothingness, despair, depression, and darkness have slowly made their state of mind the normal. Their reality is blinded by their focus—giving up. It is sometimes up to you, that friend, family member, or stranger, to turn that person's life around from total destruction. We have to let them know someone does care and will offer that ear to listen or shoulder on which to cry. However, there will be some, regardless of the words, who will not listen. God has given us the freedom of choice. What will you do with yours today? How about helping and loving thy fellow neighbor? How about the one reading this? Don't give up. Fight to get it back. I know that it is different for all of us, but make the choice to start living once again.

The question shouldn't be, "Will I be in the room?" The question should be, "Where am I going to be seated at the table?" On which seat are you working? I know where my eyes are set. Without a plan, there can be no implementation. Without implementation, there is no action. Without action, you will never achieve your goals.

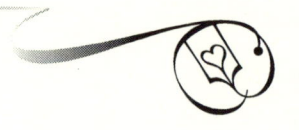

Until you stop wondering about the future, worrying about the present, and wishing you could change the past, you will never realize your potential to change the world. So today I ask, What are you going to do? Do that one thing you know you've been putting off. Make that decision to fight to keep that family intact. Get up and decide you are an overcomer. Remember no one has the power to stop you except you. Don't you give up.

Don't give in. Don't give up. Regardless of what it looks like, don't stop believing in yourself. You're not always going to be moving forward, but you're still standing for a reason. Press through, and you'll make it to your destination.

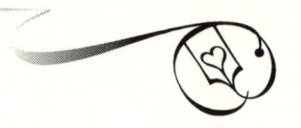

Regardless of our circumstances, we are still here for a reason. Even though you may not have made it to your destination, don't forget to reach back and help others who may be searching for direction or may have given up. You just might be the missing key to their success, which also may affect yours.

So many of us go through our lives worrying about tomorrows that may never come and thinking about the unchangeable past. And for what? It simply chokes the present. Live and enjoy your today, plan for the future, and leave the rest behind.

Before anyone else can believe in you, you must believe in yourself. Having doubt and fear is normal, but don't let them run your life. They are simply life's little tests for you to overcome. We all are meant to be overcomers. Stay in the race and keep your head up. As a motorcycle instructor, I know that regardless of how far down you think you've gotten, if you just look to where you want to go and throttle up, that bike will pull up and go in that direction. So look up, and your life will start heading in that direction.

I'm giving thanks that I woke up on the right side of the ground this morning. We have been given yet another day to get it right. Yesterday is nothing but a memory. Make that decision, put your plan in action, and quit procrastinating. There are those around you who are dying to help, but you need to take that first step. How can you be a failure if you don't quit? You're not. How can you be a success if you've never tried? Get out there today and start. Yesterday is gone, and none of us have been promised to see tomorrow. Live this day.

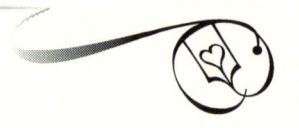

You know you're about to come out of the woods into a clearing when you hit that patch of briers. It's almost like life's sticky reminders of what you've gone through. Some will give up, never reaching their destination. They'll continue to circle, only to lose time looking for an alternate route. Others will press through, regardless of how hard the pain or test. It's time to get through those briers to our clearings.

Get rid of the deer ticks around you in the form of so-called friends. They will suck the life right out of you. If you have that negative someone who is surrounded by drama, they might be a deer tick. They will fall off anyway when you need them, as you start to walk through your storms.

It is never too late, and you are not too old for your blessing. "He shall restore the years that the locust and canker worms have eaten." Get up, get out, and don't let anyone stop you from doing what God has put in your heart to do. It's yours. It's already been done. You just have to open your eyes to see and claim it. None of us can fly with the eagles every day, but be thankful we still have the wings to get off the ground.

Stick to being more organized and better managing your time. If you're running your tail off all day, and at the end of it, you're no closer to your destination, you may want to organize, prioritize, and plan your tomorrows.

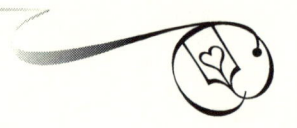

Anyone can talk about doing something, but only a few are willing to act. Just take an extra minute to knock on that door of that elderly person who lives right beside you. These are times when you truly realize the type of community in which you live. In your later years, those seeds planted will come back to you in the form of that person checking on you.

Things aren't always what they appear to be. It could be wise to get a second set of eyes or ears on the matter, before making the decision.

With every breath taken is an opportunity to put an end to that which is destroying your life, or an opportunity to start working on your dreams. Which will you choose for you and your loved ones? Why wait? There is no better time to start than right now.

Every one of us has something for which to be thankful, and not just on New Year's and Christmas but every day we take a breath of life. We should be thankful for living in a country where we have the freedom to live our lives as we please. Everything may not be all right in our lives right now, but don't give up. Your day is coming.

What will you do today that will not only affect your life but the lives of those around you as well? A couple of you out there feel as though all hope is lost and no one cares. God has given us all a purpose. Find yours. Look up, reach out your hand, and someone will be there to pull you through. A few of us are going in circles, searching, and we don't realize it. We have simply become complacent. Nothing is changing except the date on the calendar. It's time to wake up and do what you know you're supposed to be doing and be where you're supposed to be. There's a master plan for all our lives; we just have to act to tap into it.

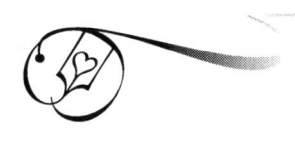

Say something kind or special to someone out of the blue. You never know what they may be going through. Yes, even that person who puts on the smiles and looks like a million bucks on the outside; they just might need that word from you. You never know just how close to the edge someone may be from their outward appearance. I can look back on my life and see those times of darkness, and no one knew just how low I was hovering. God has a plan for your life.

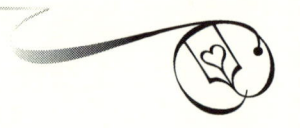

To that one hanging on by a thread, I know it seems like all hope is gone. I know it feels like no one would understand your sorrows. I know you feel like just giving up. Look up and reach out to that hand that has always been there. Make that decision and know that you are going to make it through your test and on to success. Remember you're not alone. Don't give up and don't give in. Your victory awaits.

There's a time in all our lives when we must decide to continue on the same easy path or take the more difficult road, which is only limited by our imagination. Make that decision right now to do what you know you're supposed to be doing, and stop doing what you know you're not supposed to be doing.

Time to do it again, only better and having learned from mistakes.

It's when you feel like giving up and are defeated that you have to dig in and fight for your desired results. Don't give in. Help is on the way. For some of you, just look up and grab that hand that's always been there. For others, it is simply about making the right choices that will change your life forever.

Don't wait for special days to be thankful. If you pause and think, we all have something daily for which to be thankful.

Turn that disaster or situation in your life that was supposed to cause you to give up into an opportunity. Pass your test, don't give up, and expect more.

Procrastination is enemy number one. How will it affect your life today? For some, it will be that splinter. Splinters come in many forms. Sometimes painless at first, they all can lead to infection. Pull it and throw it away. Take action and take control over your situation. No one else can do it for you.

So why does it take a near-death experience or hitting rock bottom before changing that one thing that is truly self-destructive and causing others pain as well? On the other hand, I don't think any of us would be so quick to judge after a little self-examination.

Sometimes you're given a chance of a lifetime, but your mind-set is too blind to see it. Someone has told you, "You'll never amount to anything." Quit holding yourself back and do that one thing you've kept yourself from doing. No one is going to do it for you. Get it done.

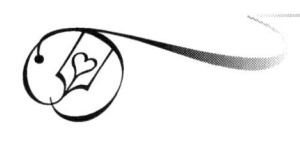

Remember the true priorities in your life. Remember your family and friends. Don't let it be said too late. What will they say about you when you're gone? What do they say about you now, when you're not in the room? Let's treat each other with respect and learn to forgive those who sometimes don't deserve it. Let's learn to communicate and disagree, without it resulting in spewing hateful remarks of disrespect. The next time you're thinking about yelling out the window at that other driver or throwing off more signals than WVU's offensive coach, try looking back over your life and remembering you weren't always perfect either. We all have made mistakes.

We can get so much more done by working together, instead of individuals we put in power working on selfish missions for themselves. "We the people" cannot forget we matter.

Carrying around stress and anger is worse than pointing a loaded weapon at yourself. The weapon won't go off unless you pull the trigger. Stress and anger don't need a trigger. The longer you carry them around, the more they destroy your life, eventually killing you in one form or another. Drop it, forgive them, move forward, and don't worry about things you cannot change. The past is the past. Let it go.

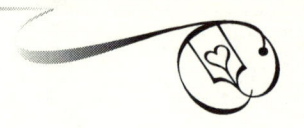

Through it all, the good times and the so-called bad, we still need to be thankful. I don't believe any of us are wondering from where our next meal will come. I know none of us are going to die from lack of water. Yes, the bills may come, or that relationship or lack thereof may get you down, but look over your life, and you will see that we all have reasons to be thankful. The best thing is the rest of our story is yet to be written, and we still have the power of choice. How will you start your next chapter?

Regardless of who has come and gone, regardless of what has happened in your life, regardless of what you think, and no matter what you have done, you are still here for a reason. Get up, give thanks, and let's get it right.

To that one who is thinking about giving up, don't. You're going to make it through. You think you're the only one going through trials. You're not. There is a plan in place for you. Hold on to your dreams and put your plan in action. My purpose was to share this message at this hour.

Don't ever stop dreaming, but it takes a well-thought-out plan to make that dream come true. I'm working on mine and hopefully will be able to eventually help others.

Instead of concentrating on past failures you cannot change, start concentrating on your present situation and how much a simple decision can change your life or those of others around you. We are all still here for a reason. Once you figure it out, nothing can keep you from attaining it but you.

Too much of a good thing can lead to destruction. We've got to have balance. Too many fish in the ship will cause it to sink. Remember to do something good for someone else—just because.

Slow down and realize that through all of our tests and trials, we are still here. Find your purpose and hold on to it. Never give up on yourself.

At times, one day at a time is all you can do. Just make sure you have checkpoints. They will assure that you are moving toward your goals and not sitting still.

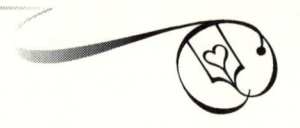

Don't be so negative and judgmental of yourself that you believe others see you the same way as you do. Often that perceived reality is what drives it to be in existence. Get up and reset your mental baseline. Folks are depending on you.

To those of you who may be in the midst of a storm, hold on and don't give up. You may have to shelter in place, but help is on the way. "Weeping may endure for the night, but ..." Do not let others determine your destiny.

*L*et go of the past so you can start enjoying your future. Regardless of how it may appear, the best is yet to come.

I can tell you, if you sit still, your situation will be unchanged. Grab the steering wheel (take control of your life), release the brake (quit worrying about what others think), hit the gas (motivate yourself), and you will make it to your destination.

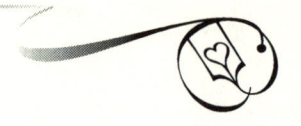

Get up, get out, and get it done. Quit putting it off … no excuses. There are some things that only we can do for ourselves or for our business. We have been allowed time to rethink, regroup, and plan. Now is the time.

More communication, less assuming, less rage, and a sincere apology can be a good start. Life is too short to stress over things that have no value, and I don't mean money.

It takes an awful lot of energy and time to hate. It also takes a toll on your body to stress over the things you cannot change or control. So upon awakening tomorrow, love more and live your life. Sometimes we need to accept that love that's right there in front of us.

Worrying won't change a thing, except your health. Work through it and do the best that you can. You may not be where you want to be, but thank God we are not where we used to be. Keep moving forward.

Today is a perfect day to stop making excuses for why you can't do something. We may never see another Monday. So let's get it started. If you are already working on it, don't give up. Joy is just around the corner. Your works have not been in vain.

They say the early bird gets the worm. They failed to mention he also gets less sleep and sometimes goes crazy. Before taking on the challenges of the day, we've got to get the proper rest and fuel.

Today, no excuses. Let it be the day you can look back on, remembering how you made that change or decision for a better life. Love and laugh more. Ask yourself why you can't be happy and satisfied with your present status. You may not have reached the stars, but you're still heading in that direction.

When will we all realize there's no use in being mean and nasty to one another? It actually takes more effort to get upset and angry than to ignore it. Do the right thing and take the high road. Also, lets quit stereotyping one another. Get to know that person before you cast judgment. None of us are perfect, and we all get old.

Regardless of how high you soar, expect a little rain in your forecast. Those who expect to constantly see the sun are those who, during a shower, forget to breathe and suffocate themselves by not being prepared for reality. Reality is life, and no one can predict what tomorrow shall bring.

Regardless of how hard it may get, even if it seems as though you're taking a step forward and getting knocked back two, regardless of the pain and confusion, regardless of that financial situation, stand, hold on, and don't give up. It's going to be all right.

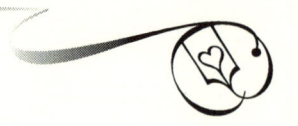

As I look back over my life, regardless of ups and downs, I'm still thankful just to have seen another day. There are those who didn't make it. We should all slow down long enough to take inventory of our lives. You'll find many reasons for which to be thankful.

What a journey life can sometimes be. You never know what's around the next corner. Just don't give up; stay on course. In the hardest of times, someone will always be there to help you through. You may not even know they are there, but they see you and your situation—real-life angels. If you can, get out today and be that angel for someone.

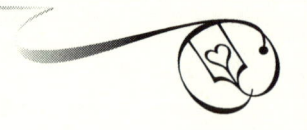

Quit living to please and keep others happy. Sometimes you have to understand it will be only you and God. You have to love and please yourself before you please and love anyone else. Someone out there today needs to buy themselves flowers or pat themselves on the back. It's going to be all right.

We all come to a point in life where we realize what we are supposed to be doing, regardless of how difficult it may be. Just don't realize it too late. Time waits for no one. Start living like never before. Some may think you've lost your mind. Just do it.

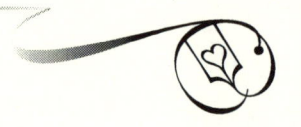

And they're off! Let's get that one thing done today—the one we've been putting off and making excuses about. For a change to take place, there are some things in your life that only you can address.

Today, someone needs to hear that you still care. Someone is masking the pain with false smiles. If that someone is reading this, you don't have to reply. Just decide to choose life. There are those who still love you. To all my fellow veterans, thank you.

Sometimes people just need someone to listen without judging. Sometimes people just need that ear to which they can vent, trusting that it won't get broadcasted as soon as they walk away. Be that someone when opportunity presents itself.

Quit blaming others for your present state. Most of the time, we made the decisions that got us there; just about all the time, we can make the decisions to get us out. It's your time to make that decision.

Sometimes you just have to dive in and get wet, for no other reason than to say you weren't afraid to take on the challenge. So today, take a walk in the rain, dive in the pool, or jump in the puddle. Reboot and take on your challenge. Don't be afraid to ask for help if it is needed, but also remember you'll have to go through some things alone. In the end, you'll be stronger.

I'm still here. I'm coming out of it. I see situations turning around. I'm actually living the chapter where it all changed forever. I can hardly wait to see the blessings in store for us; we kept believing and did not give up.

For those of you who are thinking about giving up, look to the dandelion for an example of perseverance. Less than twenty-four hours after cutting down the dandelion, it rises — above all. We have the same roots, so let's rise above it all.

Is life what you make it, or is life daily forming and making you? We can't control a lot of things in our lives. There are even going to be things that will shake our very foundation and make us question our desire to succeed and make it through. It is in these times that we will have to choose to take control of our own lives and press through.

Just remember, sometimes it's the simple things that matter the most.

If this day were your last, who would you apologize to, help, hug, or say you love? How about living this day as the first of many to come without regrets? It's time to make that decision, to take control of your future and affect others.

Last night, I woke up and saw the moon and stars. This morning, I was awakened by birds singing. Today, I've seen the sunshine and felt the drops of rain. Don't ever take the simple things in life for granted. In our worst of times, we are still blessed.

Don't fall into that trap of focusing on the negatives in your life. Know that this too shall pass. You haven't gotten this far—and some of you, survived this long—only to be destroyed by that one thing, that one person, that financial problem. Remember misery loves company. Ignore it, move past it, and get away from that which is bringing you down. If you have to, turn on your own light within to brighten your day.

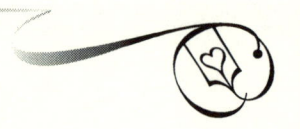

If you started yesterday and liked the results, duplicate it. It's just that simple. Start expecting more out of yourself and your life.

Ready ... set ... go! Less talk today and more action. There are no limits to what we can accomplish once we set our minds to do it.

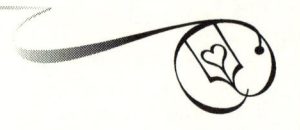

As I sit here in raw silence, only hearing the residue of a train's whistle in the distance, I am thankful. I haven't made it to where I'm going, but I can look back from where I've come. We all have a purpose. Find yours and embrace it.

We've all been blessed with yet another day. Instead of dreading it, or if you're unhappy with your present situation, what will you do to change it? Don't wait for someone else to do what you can do yourself. Get up, get out, and get it done.

Sometimes you just have to dance. A kind word to someone or a smile won't hurt either. A little serving of laughter on the side will also brighten the moment. Respect and love one another. Just a few ingredients for a better tomorrow.

I saw a tree today in the neighborhood. A storm had ripped off every large branch. Yet, a small branch extended from within and displayed beautiful flowering blooms. What will shine through in your life when you've been battered and beaten?

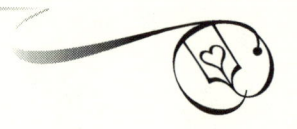

It's a good day to repair that relationship with an old friend. It doesn't matter who's at fault. It's been so long; some have forgotten why you stopped talking in the first place. Grow up and get over it. Yes, they hurt your feelings, but it's time to reach out and repair. Do it before it's too late.

You'll never see your blessings while walking around with your head down. Look up. No one else is to blame for you remaining in your current status but you. It won't be easy, but only you can change it.

The things that happen and people who frustrate us most just may be a blessing in disguise. Instead of automatically reacting in anger, think twice about what happened. Usually, if you remain still, you will realize there was a purpose in it all happening that way. Don't be so frustrated and miss it.

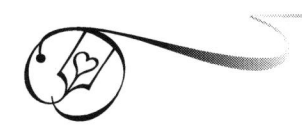

We are like vehicles. The older we get, the more miles we put on our bodies, and the more dings and dents we acquire. Some of us even get a complete overhaul, but through it all, we can still carry our load.

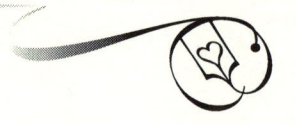

Good morning, folks. It's a brand-new day to start or complete that one thing you've been putting off day after day. No excuses. It'll take some work, but you can do it. Later, I hope to get some good reports. For me, it was this book. What have you been putting off?

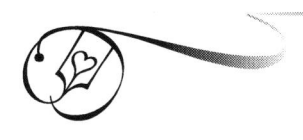

Just maybe if I'm up and out early enough, I'll miss the morning traffic. So, good morning and have a wonderful day. Change your routine if you want different results. Remember, if you already know arrival times with traffic, you can't blame it for being late.

Every now and then, you need to take time out for yourself. Listen to music, play it, or write it. Smile and say hello to that stranger. Do something special for that loved one in your life to show them that you still care. There are too many assumptions these days. Tomorrow is not promised to any of us. Live with no regrets.

What will you do with your tomorrow? Will you reach out and lend a helping hand? Will you whisper a kind word to a perfect stranger? Whatever it may be, make it count.

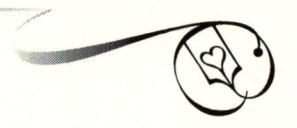

Determined and expecting more. Enough said.

Sometimes we don't realize that in so many ways, we do have control over our future. It's in the choices that we've made and the seeds that are sown throughout our past and future. What shall be your next choice for tomorrow?

Don't you spend another moment thinking about the pain and trials of yesterdays. Don't get caught up and stress about what is yet to come. Let go and live this day, for tomorrow is not promised to any of us. Get up, get out, and stay focused on that goal. It's closer than you think.

If we can't get it right today, or at least get started in that direction, we never will. No excuses. Get it done, step out of the box, and do something about it.

Do you ever have those nights when the brain just won't slow down, thinking about what great things are to come? It almost feels like that night before Christmas. I don't know what's coming, but there's a harvest for those of us who have put in the hours and believed.

If you're reading this, then you have a purpose to fulfill. I can't tell you what it is, but I can guess that it's very important that you do it. It will be all right. I've done my part.

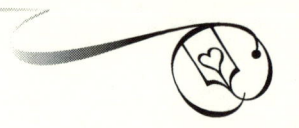

Seek happiness, and it shall eventually find you. Dwell on the past, and it will consume your very soul. Start expecting and knowing that a brighter day is coming for you and yours. Just hang in there and be patient.

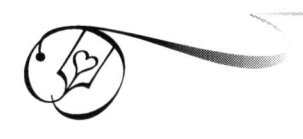

Sometimes you just have to be still and know that weeping may endure for a night, but joy and your help come in the morning. Be still and be patient. Your work, your prayers, and your advice in that situation were not in vain. It's going to be more than just all right. Expect more.

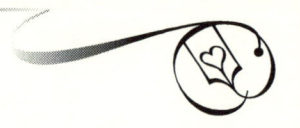

This year, what do you want to get accomplished? Is there a relationship to mend? Is there a business you need to start? Is there someone you need to put out of your life? Will you help someone, just because you can? Each one of us is born with certain talents and keys. Start using them.

You cannot change another person. They have to want it for themselves and be strong enough to change their "just one more" to "no more!" Then you will see the change taking place not only in their lives but in those around them. We all have room for improvement.

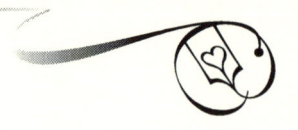

The ones who love will be there in the good times and the bad. They will have faith in you even when you've lost faith or hope in yourself. Take inventory of your so-called friends and make sure they don't cloud up your priorities to love the ones who love you.

You know it's so easy being thankful in the good times. The true test is being thankful even in the bad times. Your faith will be followed by your blessings.

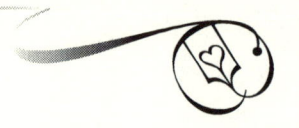

Life is too short not to forgive one another. Regardless of who was at fault, it takes both of you to make the decision to move forward. I know some will disagree with this, but none of us are perfect. Once we all realize we can eliminate a whole lot of drama, gossiping, and hating on one another, life will instantly become better.

Some of us can only see as darkness falls upon our lives. Don't wait for the darkness but seek while light still shines all about your life. When darkness comes, it's always a journey to get back to the light. It didn't happen overnight; nor will it be fixed in an instant. God has given us all gifts. Use them.

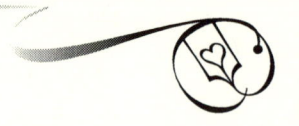

Instead of delivering unforgettable cuts to the heart, it is wise to hold one's tongue. An angered person sometimes speaks loudest with silence.

To be consumed by darkness and wetness one night and to wake to a blanket of whiteness the next morning kind of makes you wonder who's really in control. I know most of us reading this have control over our lives and the freedom of choice, but I believe God has a bigger purpose for each one of us.

Life ... live it. Don't let it live you. Regardless of how the situation appears, don't give up on yourself. Expect more.

For those of us who are sinking in quicksand, God sends us ladders, ropes, and tree branches to grab, but instead, we keep asking for oxygen tanks with which to breathe, consumed by the darkness of our self-made realities.

Your answered prayer may not be in the form you thought it would come. It may be that something that has been there, standing by for you to notice it. So the next time you pray, you may want to ask for vision to see the many blessings that are right in front of you.

I will ... I can ... I shall ... I'm going to ... It's up to you to fill in the rest. None of us have a predetermined destiny. The one thing in life that can change your tomorrows, and that no one can take away, is choice. Start believing in yourself instead of waiting for someone else's approval.

Positive thinking and good thoughts are merely words unless you also take corrective actions. So, get up, get out, and do what you're supposed to be doing. No one can do it but you.

It's a new day. What are you doing with it? You're here for a reason. You are someone special. Start doing that thing that you have been led to do but are afraid to do. Expect more and know—not *think*—it will work out for you in ways you never imagined.

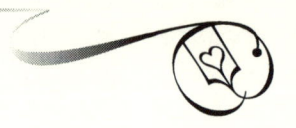

The greater the test and trial, the greater the blessing on the other side, and I'm not talking about after death. Our blessing is just around the corner. Stand firm, expect, and believe that yours is on the way. We've come too far to give up now. Keep working toward your goal. Again, don't give up.

What will be the product of your harvest? Are you sowing your seeds in the right place? How can you expect so much when you've sacrificed so little? It's not too late to make that change. Let's get it right today—just one day at a time, knowing that relaxation, rest, and happiness will come.

What will you do differently this week to affect your future? Is it leaving that job for another uncertain future of running your own business? Is it asking that one out you've been afraid to ask out for so long? Is it leaving that one you know you should have left years ago? This week, make a decision.

Always remember that a little bit of something is much better than all, or a whole lot of nothing, and no, life isn't always fair.

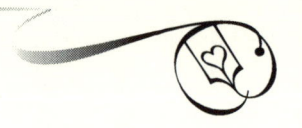

That very person you talk about, hate on, and spread vicious rumors about just may be the very person who makes the decision tomorrow that forever affects your life. Life is too short. Love one another, or at least respect one another. We've got to quit blaming others for our own failures. Don't quit because of what someone else didn't do for you.

Regardless of our plans, tomorrow is not promised to any of us. Live this day, enjoy your loved ones, and forgive those you said you'll forever hate. If you're sick, refuse that bad report, take your next breath, and don't let anyone put a shutdown time on your life. We've got to start getting along and looking out for one another. Life is too short to do otherwise.

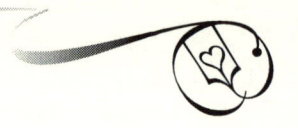

If you continue down the tunnel, only looking for the light at the end of it, you may just miss all the blessings along the way. Even in our struggles, we are blessed to see another day. It's a blessing just to be able to get out of the bed in the morning. Sometimes it's simply about lifting your head and noticing the emergency exits above and around you.

Today, don't accept anything less than a yes. Open and walk through the doorway before you and don't look back. Yesterday is yesterday for a reason. You'll have your haters, which are normally those closest to you, but don't give in to their negativity. Sometimes we have to walk through that door alone. Get up and claim what has always been yours.

At the end of the day, you've got to get in sync with your purpose in life. Until the two of you meet, it will always seem that you are caught in a struggle. Your true purpose may not be in alignment with your future plans. Most of the time, it will be a test of faith, but keep common sense in play. Once you're in alignment with your true purpose, the rest will fall into place.

Just remember as you go through your tests and trials, a feast is usually preceded by famine. So, as you go through that dry spell, just keep on planting. Keep on removing those weeds from around you. (You know who they are.) Stay the course and know that your closed doors will open unto a harvest and feast that's more than enough for you.

Sometimes we get so caught up and concerned about our own problems that we forget about others who are going through their own trials as well. Even in our times of tests and trials, we can still reach out and help others along the way. That very person you helped may be the one who eventually keeps you from drowning. Love one another.

Have you ever slowed down and wondered who you really are? What have you done that will be remembered long after you're gone? It makes me think about my father's deeds. I still have people approaching me about him and telling me stories of how he affected their lives. I can only hope that people will do the same when I'm gone. Love thy neighbor.

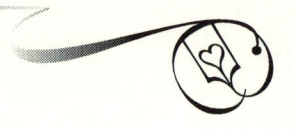

Have you stopped to think about the lives sacrificed for our freedom? Men and women have given the ultimate sacrifice for all of us who are reading this right now. All of our families have been touched one way or another by veterans and those who are on active duty. If you see or know a veteran, thank them for their service to this great country.

I was wondering today why it seems so easy for others, but then I realized I don't know their story. Someone has put in the sacrifices, hard work, and time to make it work. So, as I look back through my several failed attempts at financial success, I realize it doesn't come overnight or in a lotto ticket. I've got to work through the circumstances given unto me and make it.

When will we all realize that true success is having the ability to help someone else achieve their success? The ultimate goal is for these actions to multiply, affecting even those who were not thinking about their next move toward success. A word of encouragement doesn't cost a thing.

Don't let all this gloomy grayness affect your chi/qi. Get out and do something that's going to have a positive effect on your life. I know sometimes we have to be still, but that only comes after we've made every God-given effort to do something about our situation. Trust me. Have a little more faith, expect it, and watch it all fall into place.

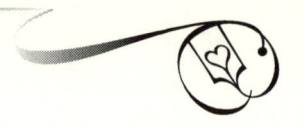

What price would you pay to help out a complete stranger? I've found out that the more you give, the more that is given unto you. Next time you give, look at your motivation. Is it because you want someone to sing your praises? If so, they will never be enough. If it is truly from the heart, almost in that instant, it will come back to you multiplied.

Sometimes you just have to run those red lights that life presents you. You'll have to walk it alone sometimes, but in the end and for not giving up, your reward shall be worth it. Don't ever give up, keep the faith, and don't let anyone tell you that you're not going to make it. Expect more.

Let us not wait for yet another tragedy to bring us together as a family, community, state, or country. I'm tired of some folks thinking about others only during a moment of tragedy. Let's work on loving one another in the good times and the bad. Each of us has our own individual part to play in building a stronger unified tomorrow for us all. What's yours?

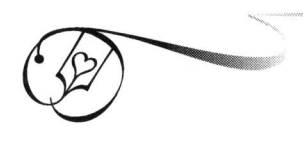

I'm thankful to have my health and the ability to work on my goals in life. There are some who will not see another tomorrow. There are those who will not be able to say another goodnight. Today, be thankful for what you've got. If you need motivation, look back at your life and struggles, the mountains over which you've come. Don't give up.

"One more ..." How many times have you said it? In your life, to what does it relate? If it is a positive thing, bravo, but if it is negatively affecting your life and loved ones, now is the time to quit.

Regardless of how you look at your situation, be thankful. We all have lots for which to be thankful. It may not be the way we think it should be right now, but still, it's not what it used to be. We've still got fight left in us to make changes in our lives, our families, our communities, our states, and the world. For whom shall you make that change?

Stay on course, finish the race, get up, keep fighting, keep moving forward, don't ever give up. I know these trials can wear you down at times, but be still and hold on. Just when you think it's over, someone will step in and show you why you kept the faith. It's only a test. We will make it through.

I believe there's a blessing around the corner, because this has surely been my month of Job. Tests and trials on every hand simply means there's a bigger blessing on the other side of this moment in time. I'm believing, knocking down doors, expecting, working, praying, and trusting all will work out. Stand by for one heck of a testimony.

We can either help and bring a solution to the table or quit blocking those who are trying to get it done, whose ideas may be a little different from ours. Complaining does nothing, and precious time is wasted, and then you wonder why you're in the same situation. Today, if you want different results, get up, get out, and work on changing it.

Today is a new day—another day and opportunity for us to start it, work on it, finish it, or sit and watch the time pass us by. I'm going to start my new year right now and work on some things. How about you?

It's time to get it done. No waiting around to get some type of justification from someone who doesn't give a crap about you or your situation. Change for the better is right there waiting for you to make a decision. Do it and expect more. No use waiting for the new year to do what you can do today.

My goodness, sometimes you just don't realize how tired you were until you're once again rested. I believe I've been sleepwalking for the past thirty days. So, I apologize if I haven't returned a call or two. I've found even Batman needs a little rest every now and then. I've rebooted the system and am ready to have a strong finish to this year. Expect more.

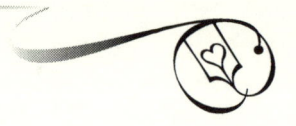

At the end of the day, when all the lights and glitter are gone, when all the money and fancy outings have dried up, when you have nothing left to give, your true friends will reveal themselves. Even though it's been a while since you last spoke, they've been there waiting for you to realize they never left your side. It was you who closed the door. Open it.

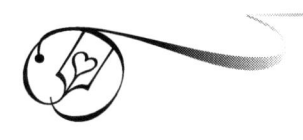

Sometimes in life you have to create your own opportunity instead of complaining about when it will come. Expect more and keep working on it. You'll make it.

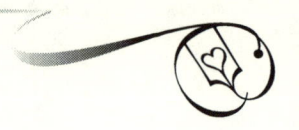

𝓔ventually, you come to the conclusion that our lives here on earth are limited. We cannot slow or stop the hands of time. How will you be remembered? What mark will you leave on the people around you? Live without regrets, laugh and smile more, give a hug or two, and take time for yourself every now and then.

Even though the clouds seem like they have been with us for a while, the sun still shines brightly. The clouds in our lives will eventually burn off and reveal the blessing that's always been there. You simply need to rise up to receive it and quit holding your head down. Just as in motorcycling, your bike goes where you look, so start looking up toward your blessing.

Let's all do something nice for someone we don't even know, or better yet someone who doesn't like us, without expecting anything back. Trust me; your blessing will burst through the door to get back to you.

Just hang on. You'll make it to your next destination. I say next destination because when you stop making new goals for yourself, I believe you stop living. We won't get it all done, but it's nice to get to a place where we can look back and know we gave it an honest try. So be happy where you are in life. Don't complain if you're not trying to do something about it.

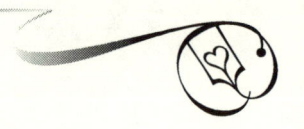

You will never fail if you never give up. You may not achieve what you set out to accomplish the first or even the third or fourth time. I know this from my own life. Don't give up. I haven't made it to where I want to be, but I'm not where I used to be. You'll know you're getting close when folks start talking about you behind your back. Pray for them and move on.

I believe some of us have gone through a storm over the past few months. Get ready for some new growth and prosperity. Let's expect more of God's favor in our lives. Find your purpose and don't let anyone get in your way.

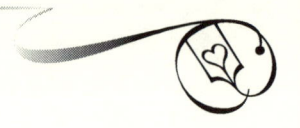

Does it ever stop? Not until you're six feet under. The only question is, What in your life do you want to stop? You've got to make the decision to change it. No one else can do it for you, especially the ones who love you most. It's time for it to stop and for you to take your blessings right there in front of you. It's time to live.

Take time to evaluate your mental and physical wellness. As I've burned the candle from both ends this past year, trying to play catchup, I've realized the importance of listening to my body. We can't help anyone from a hospital bed. So, as I say to others who are operating in superhero mode, slow down and rest every now and then. The world will go on with or without us.

I do hope you can look back on your journey and realize you may not be where you want to be, but you're sure not where you used to be. Unlike a train, we have the ability to change tracks, paths, and direction. Make the change today that will forever affect your life and those of others around you for the good. Don't ever give up. We are almost there, my friends.

At the end of the day, who are you tucking in? Who is laying their head down beside of you? Just remember it's the little things that count the most. There are no redos in life. Get it right, regardless of how many failures there have been.

The right time is when you make it the right time for yourself to move on and start living again. I know it's hard when that person has been your world and for whom you have lived, but you're still here for a reason. Whatever the case may be, quit the blame game and what-ifs and find yourself. You deserve to be happy. Don't you give up, and allow yourself time to heal.

If you can help someone else today achieve their dreams, do it. It all comes around. You may think your life is upside down, but the true blessing is being able to give or being in a position to help others. Eventually, we all experience one side or the other of a need or blessing. Together, each in our own way, we will make a difference. Don't give up.

Although it's gloomy, the sun is still shining. Just as in our lives, we may experience our downtimes, but hold on for that brighter day. Your strength shall be renewed, and you'll be able to accomplish and endure the rest of your journey. No one said it would be easy. Just complete your task at hand even though you can't see the results. They're coming.

Get up today and start doing what you've been destined to do. You don't need to be told what you already know. The doors are unlocked. You just have to push them open and walk through. Expect more.

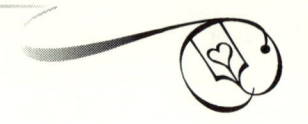

"It is what it is" is wearing me out. It is a true statement only if you accept and believe it. I refuse to accept it. I'm believing for more in my life. It is what you choose to believe. It is and forever will be changes toward the good, if only you expect more. I believe we are just around the corner from claiming our blessings. Just a little bit farther. Don't you give up now.

Have you really ever thought about the rain and tears? It is through them life is sometimes given, they both have a cleansing effect, and they usually set a precedent to new beginnings. Sometimes we need to shed those tears of sorrow and helplessness. Just don't stay in that place. You have to get up, stand up, and fight. Your blessing awaits just on the other side.

As you and your loved ones settle in for bed, remember those who are less fortunate than you and I. Some people would kill just to have our bad days. I know we all get down sometimes and feel like breaking in two, but even then, we are blessed. We still have choices in our lives. Tomorrow, what choice will you make that will eventually change your future?

That which we are focused on the most will become our daily reality. If we focus on our problems, they will consume our minds. Focus on that one thing you want the most in your life and work toward it, moving and kicking anything out of the way that tries to hinder your success. Stop complaining about your current situation and do something about it. Don't you ever give up.

Just remember these two things when you think your life is so bad. First, there is someone praying to have it as good as you; your situation could be much worse. Second, you still have your life and are able to complain. There are those who will not wake up this morning. Even through our own tests and trials, be thankful. We are truly blessed. Don't you give up on you.

This day holds different things for each one of us, but it's up to you individually to go out, find it, and grab it. You will accomplish nothing by just sitting there and asking, "Why me?" or "Why this situation?" or "Why ..." Make this day your day, one to remember for a lifetime. Instead of whys, how about, "I *will* start, get, do, and accomplish"?

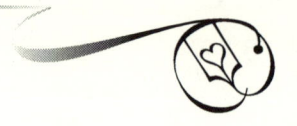

Try and try again until you get it right. If it doesn't work, try harder. Eventually you will succeed. Sometimes a little more effort and a plan are the only things holding you back from your hopes and dreams. Go into tomorrow knowing that it's a new day. It will be remembered as the day you took that first step on a new path toward your blessings. Expect more and believe it.

Just remember, all of us are on that road to success if we work hard and stay focused. We are just at different mile markers. I'll see you when I get there, and oh the story we will be able to tell of how we made it through.

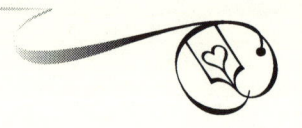

Time waits on no one. Get up, fight for what you want, and quit being an observer of life around you. Be a participant in your life's destiny. We all have been blessed with the ability to choose. Granted, not all of mine have been the best every time, but they were my choices. Choose this day to do it differently and expect more out of life. Believe it and know it'll come.

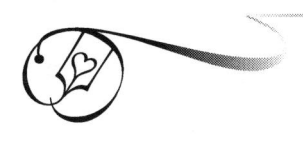

I was reminded this morning that there are several of us still going through our own version of hell on earth. It is in these times when those helping hands can make a difference. Some will spray water on the flames, and others will take the risk of reaching into the fire to pull you out of that situation. I have experienced both in my life.

There's no time like the present to finish what you started. There's no time like the present to accomplish that goal. There's no time like the present to start building something from the foundation up. Don't let anyone tell you that you're too old or too young to do it. We may not make it together, but I'll see you at the finish line.

After you get through all of your tests and trials, don't be surprised if that very person you thought was a friend is driving a knife through your back and hating on you, because you're able to stand on your own. They were not a true friend. On the other side of the coin, don't forget those who have helped you achieve your success.

When it seems no one can understand your sorrows and trials, when you wear a smile on your face, but behind closed doors you're struggling just to breathe, stand firm and know you will make it through. Stand and know your purpose will be revealed unto you. Your trials will turn into testimonies, and your smiles shall be true. Stand firm through your test.

After all the balls are thrown and the champions are in front of us, we all have to again start working on our own Super Bowls in our personal lives. No one will hand you a trophy, and no one will announce it on FOX or CNN. Sometimes, no one but you will even notice that you've won your Super Bowl. Keep on pressing toward that goal line. You'll make it.

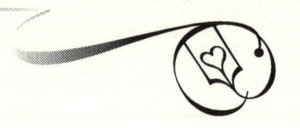

There's an old black spiritual that says, "Don't let the devil ride." That devil in your life can come in many forms. It can be a financial burden, problems with a loved one, an addiction, or depression that's taken over your life. Whatever it is, kick it out of your car and plot a new direction. Just follow the signs, and you'll make it to your destination.

They've said, "Almost heaven." I'm going to get out this morning and work on my piece of it. It's not going to be handed to you. You've got to go and find it and work for it, and it shall be given to you. Sometimes you're waiting at the door, and it won't open. Knock it off its hinges and go get the blessing that awaits you. It's yours. Don't you ever give up.

It's time to believe. Believe things will get better and believe this time it will work. Believe and have faith that you and yours will make it through, regardless of how that situation you're in looks. Even though others may write you off, don't you ever give up on you.

Always remember you have a choice. As long as you are breathing and have blood running through your veins, you have a choice. Don't let anyone tell you any different. It's a choice to go after that dream, a choice to let go of ego and repair that relationship, a choice to love again. Tomorrow is not promised to any one of us. Stop holding on to the past and live again.

There's one thing to remember along the way. By ourselves, we are just a puzzle piece. You may want for nothing, and you may have several titles in front of your name and on your wall, but you're still just one piece of the puzzle, which can be replaced. It is only when we stand together that we truly have unlimited power. Together we can make a difference.

Sometimes you just have to hang in there, even when you think it's over. Keep believing and standing. Sometimes you have to stand alone, but stand and push through to the end. There's nothing wrong with resting, but do not become complacent. Stick to your plan and strive to achieve that goal. Remember, you have to believe and know that everything is going to be all right.

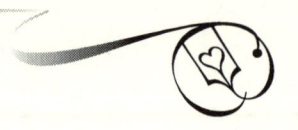

Actions without words are far better than words without actions. That's my opinion. There will be plenty of time to talk about it but only a certain window of opportunity to work on it. We all have needs. Be happy for someone when they are finally blessed with opportunity or the person for which they were searching. It all comes around.

It's a good time to start doing it differently and see if you get desired results, if it hasn't been working the way you've been doing it. This means that relationship, financial investments, friends, mental health, physical health, and more. The first step is making up your mind and deciding to do it. Create and stick to your plan, allow room for alternative routes, and you'll make it.

Even though it's gloomy and you can't see it, the sun is still shining brightly. Remember, just because you can't see your blessing doesn't mean it's not there or coming your way. It's sometimes a simple test of your faith. Keep on believing and expecting your own blessing or miracle and know that's it's on the way. In spite of the obstacle before you, don't you give up.

Every now and then, I look back over my life. Where would I be if I hadn't made certain decisions? I think about the choices I've made, the hard work and prayers that have gotten me this far. I'm excited about what's coming around the corner. I'm expecting more. I'm expecting a blessing that will run over, affecting the lives of others. Don't ever give up on your dreams.

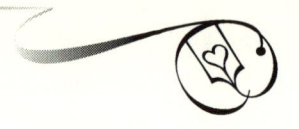

As I saw sun's rays piercing through the blanket of morning fog, I realized how thankful I should be for a new day. I'm still here and able to fight a good fight. I'm still here and able to make choices that will affect my life and others. I may not have everything I want. I may not be where I want to be, but I'm here. We have what we need inside to make it through. Don't give up.

I've got to keep going and make it to the finish line with my family. Why gain some of life's best pleasures only to turn around and see that you've lost your family through your chosen journey? When it comes down to it, it is a choice to work for more or to be comfortable in your present status. Whatever your decision, just know that family is going through hard times as well.

It's when you get tired and feel like giving up. It's when you have to steal away to your own place of stillness, because you can't wear that fake smile and hold yourself together. It's when it feels like all hope is gone, and you don't know how you're going to make it to the next day, or sometimes to the next hour. That's when you know your blessing is on the way. Don't ever give up.

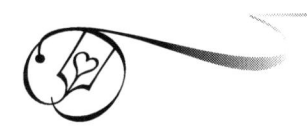

"He who is without vision imprisons himself, going through life unchanging. He who is without hope, is already dead" (*Hook Line & Single*).

ℒife. It is our choice to live it without regrets. There are no do-overs or rewind buttons, though there is a fast-forward for those who are living recklessly. Hit play and enjoy yourself and those around you. Just don't forget to hit pause every now and then to reflect and regroup. Sometimes you need to look back just to see how far you've come. Don't ever give up on your dreams.

Expectations are coming through. Just keep believing. Don't you give up on yourself. Know that's it's got to change for the good before it happens. There's no testimony without a test. Push through this thing that's got a hold of your mind, body, or finances. I'm going to go out on this ledge where I'll lose some of you, but some of you are going through a spiritual battle.

Let's expect something great to happen today. I figure if we all believe as one, something has got to happen. I remember reading where two or three shall agree, it shall be done. I'm not saying I'm putting it to the test, but let's believe for that family problem, that financial situation, that drug problem, that relationship, our community, and our country. Expect your blessing this day.

There are days you can look back on, wondering, *How in the world did I get through that day?* It is in those times when the battles are won. It is in those times that your faith is tested. I'm living that test of faith at this moment of my life. I just can't wait to be able to share my personal story. I know one thing for certain. We haven't come this far to give up now.

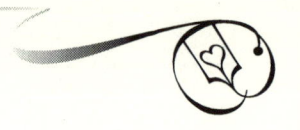

It has to get better if you keep on pushing through. Don't give in and don't give up. Joseph was sold off by his brothers, but in the end, it was he who would deliver them out of starvation and give them the riches of Egypt. Just remember to treat people right and fair. You never know what the future holds, but I do believe it all comes back around.

It's time for a real change. It's time for the chains to be broken in that situation. It's time for you to go to that next level. It's time for us to realize we can't do it by ourselves, but together we can make a difference out there. It's time to expect more. Live it, believe it, and receive it. All you have to do is believe that it's already done and rejoice about it. Have faith.

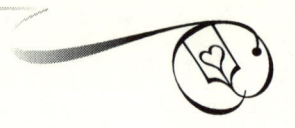

As each day passes, we get closer to either our defeat or victory. Don't give up. Stand and stay in the race. Sometimes you have to stand alone, especially when it comes to what is right. Sometimes you have to decide for yourself what is best for you. You've sought, and you've asked. Now walk through the open door and get what is yours.

It's time to get up. Get it done, because no one is going to do it for you. Faith and a little bit of work on our part goes a long way. Have a great day.

*J*ust remember, whatever it is you're going through, "This too shall pass." It's going to be all right. Once you've overcome your battle, help someone who is going through theirs and needs a helping hand. There is nothing in this world like helping someone else make it through and succeed with their dreams.

Do you ever stop and take an inventory of who would really be there for you? Every now and then, say to that one, "Thank you," or that you love them. Even though some of you don't call them unless you're in need, they're okay with that and understand. We all play roles in lives of others. The only differences are the perceptions of reality put on that relationship by each involved party. We are all here for but a time.

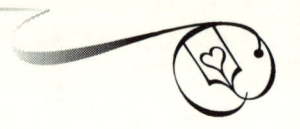

Every now and then, we've got to ask ourselves, Have we given it all we've got? Have we run a good race? Have we helped someone along the way to make their dreams come true? If you haven't thus far, don't worry; you still have time. It's your choice to make, which path you will travel through your life. Start living and quit worrying about what others think. Remember all things are possible.

Regardless of how bad we think our situation is, it could always be worse. If you're able to read this, you're blessed. We are blessed with the joy of living. While we are still able, let's bless someone else with a kind act or word of encouragement.

It's another day. Always remember, during those bad times in your relationship, you're the one who's laying your head down with him or her at night. Also, do yourself, your friends, and your family a favor and quit throwing your partner under the bus, especially if deep inside you know you still want it to work. There's nothing wrong with having an ear to talk with, but just be careful of what you're talking about.

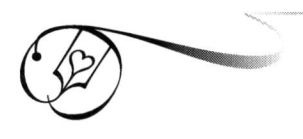

Sometimes it's best to stay away from someone who's drowning, if you're not such a good swimmer yourself.

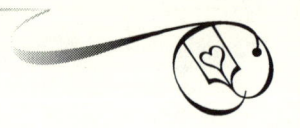

No more excuses. I'm going for it. At times, you will have to walk your road alone. Stay on course and be determined. In spite of what you see, things will work out if you believe. For the few of you who hate on others while they are fighting their battle, try putting that energy into helping them. A word of encouragement goes a long way. You'll feel a whole lot better.

Even though some things appear to be over, don't accept it. It's not over. You've just begun to live. Everything we've been going through is just a test and training of our faithfulness. We could have made the obituary pages, but we are here. What's your true purpose in life? Find it. Look beyond your present circumstances and know that it is going to be all right.

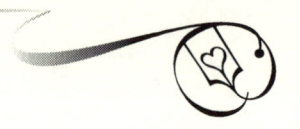

I know we all have our tests and trials, some harder than others. I also know if we can hang in there long enough, fight a good fight, and stay focused, we shall make it through. Sometimes you have to climb life's mountains, but eventually you'll be able to walk right through them.

I pray that someone will have their breakthrough today. You know who you are. I'm still working on mine, but I know it's coming. For others, sometimes you just need to be still, mentally and physically. The work has already been done. I've heard it in church for years, "Be still and know that I am God."

Today's choices will determine whether or not we realize that behind the gloom, the sun still shines brightly. We sometimes have to mentally take ourselves beyond the gloom that surrounds us and become our own light. In short, sometimes we have to stand on our own and seek that light within ourselves. Never give up on yourself. Keep striving.

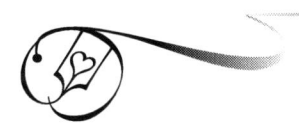

I'm proud of all of you who have made changes in your life and are doing a whole lot better now. (Kids and adults, you know who you are.) It doesn't go unnoticed. Keep your head up and continue to strive for excellence.

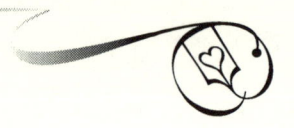

It's just nice to know there are still folks out there who care about others and are willing to lend a helping hand. Just remember folks have to eat and have needs throughout the year, even if it's not considered a holiday. Take care.

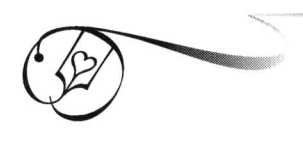

Every now and then, I must pause and know that I shouldn't complain about not having this or that. I could be homeless. My kids could be sick. My utilities could be shut off. I could be riding a bus and searching for a job. We are all blessed in several ways. It could be worse. Meanwhile, let's do something about making it to the next level.

Let's get something done today. I'm tired of working more and having less. I'm sure my tilling of the ground will soon pay off, but for now, I'm living that part of every successful entrepreneur's story of going through the storm. I'm constantly believing it shall be all right. I'm staying focused and helping anyone I can help along the way. Stay focused and keep climbing.

Now and then, it's good to pause in our pursuit of happiness and just be happy and thankful for all that we have thus far. To my true friends, I say thanks for being there, even when you didn't know. To my enemies and haters, thanks for the tests and motivation in my life. You've made me a stronger man. I pray you find something positive into which you can put all of that energy.

I can see the light at the end of the tunnel. I just hope and pray I can stay on track to get there. I've had some obstacles thrown all about this week, but I'm still closer and will keep fighting to get the job done.

Life's tests. I believe we all go through them. The question is, Are you passing them? It seems the harder they are, the bigger the blessings if you pass. Take care out there and know that, in so many ways, you're not alone.

How dedicated are you? You are successful already. You just have to realize it for yourself. Ask yourself who you will be in five and twenty years.

If you continually focus on your failures, you will become consistent at failing. Look towards success and it will find you.

ABOUT THE AUTHOR

Duke Jordan served 4 years in the US Marine Corp, retired as a Lieutenant from Charleston Police Department, and worked as contract Terrorist Scenario Planner for Homeland Response Forces. He presently sells Commercial Real Estate for Berkshire Hathaway HS GER. He has become known for his positive post on social media and continued advocate of bringing more businesses to West Virginia.

Made in the USA
Columbia, SC
07 December 2024